A DAD JOKE A DAY

DEAR _____

_____

_____

_____

_____

FROM _____

TWO SPECIAL GIFTS FOR OUR READERS

AS A SPECIAL THANK YOU FOR GETTING THIS BOOK, WE'D LIKE TO GIVE YOU:

New Message

To: theluckyreader@message.com

Subject: Dad Joke of the Day!

WHY DID THE GOLFER CHANGE HIS PANTS?

BECAUSE HE GOT A HOLE IN ONE!

A BONUS MONTH OF DAD JOKES

AN EXTRA 31 DAYS WORTH OF DAD JOKES, DELIVERED STRAIGHT TO YOUR INBOX FOR YOU TO USE ON YOUR UNSUSPECTING VICTIM!

+

A BOOK EXCLUSIVE (AVAILABLE ONLY WITH THIS BOOK)

THE SURPRISING PSYCHOLOGY OF LAUGHTER, AND 10 UNIQUE TOOLS & TECHNIQUES FOR YOU TO MAKE LAUGHTER AN EVERYDAY HABIT FOR THE FAMILY

A LAUGH A DAY

THE SURPRISING BENEFITS OF LAUGHTER AND HOW TO CREATE LAUGHTER EVERYDAY FOR THE FAMILY

VISIT WWW.DADDILIFE.COM/LOL TO GET YOURS!

TABLE OF CONTENTS

INTRODUCTION

Ah, there's nothing quite as satisfying as seeing the reaction of your beloved children as they cringe with admiration and laughter from your perfectly delivered dad joke. Whether it's the all-encompassing laugh of a little one, or the confused look of a tween trying to figure out the punchline, when that cringe is followed by an eye roll and an eventual giggle... Well, that's when you know your dad points have well and truly been won!

Welcome to A Dad Joke A Day!

This is your dad joke bible. Study it. Cherish it. Heck, go all out and worship it.

It will guarantee you hours of fun with your family and make you the certified Funny Dad of The Year (without the actual certificate!).

This is the source of your dad joke powers, and your family will wonder how on earth you're coming up with a new joke every day. For those special ones you want to let into the secret of your dad joke originality - this book is your secret ~~sauce~~ source (ba-da-boom!).

In this book, you'll find 366 of the funniest, cringiest, and most 'daddiest' of dad jokes (because we've got leap years covered too!). We also look at the surprising psychology of the dad joke, and find out from our dad community exactly how you should be telling a dad joke to guarantee success. There's an art to joke-telling that takes it from mediocre to 'full-on dad joke' levels.

WHO ARE DADDILIFE BOOKS AND WHY THIS BOOK?

This book has been written by DaddiLife Books.

DaddiLife is an online community of more than 150,000 dads from around the world sharing stories, advice, guides, and interviews that shine a light on what it means to be a modern-day dad.

Check us out at www.daddilife.com

We're a team of more than 50 writers who have been telling dad jokes to all our kids since 2014, and have tested every single one of the 366 in this bible on our own real-live subjects, whether they signed up for it or not. We didn't try any of them on animals, though. That goes against our ethics, and they wouldn't understand them anyway.

Here are a couple of real-life reactions to some of the jokes you'll find in this book, which assured us we hit the dad joke sweet spot with this book:

Jasper (5): "Noooooooo!" *and then he ran away down the corridor with his hands in the air*
Kitty (7): "Daddy, you're embarrassing. You're NOT funny!" and then she paused and gave me a hug and said, "but I do love you."
Sarah (39): "Do you REALLY have to inflict misery on other people's kids? I'm only joking, I know I poke fun about your dad jokes, but I find it kinda cute. It's pretty endearing!

Now that you've made the bold step of opening this book, it's time to settle down, prepare, and rest. For the following two chapters go into the science behind dad jokes and how best to tell them. Then you will be ready to deliver a year's worth of the best, funniest, and most cringe-worthy dad jokes to the ones you love most.

After all, this is a big step in realizing your birthright as a dad. You're a good man and a doting father. It's time to take what is yours and unleash the Dad Joke Master that has been lying in wait, deep inside of you.

God help us all! ;-)

THE SCIENCE
OF THE DAD
JOKE

So what do we know about the science and psychology of the dad joke?

A CULTURAL PHENOMENON

It's become a popular topic of debate in recent years as dad jokes appear to be going through a period of renaissance. The internet is showing a renewed appreciation and love of the dad joke, and more than one million people now subscribe to the Reddit page r/dadjokes.

Dad Jokes have spawned hugely popular online video series, often pitting comedians and celebrities against each other in a 'you laugh you lose' style stand-off. The appearance of Hollywood actors Will Ferrell and Mark Wahlberg on the Dad Jokes YouTube channel has amassed more than 33 million views. If you haven't seen it, it's well worth checking out!

In fact, if there is anything that shows us that the dad joke is all the rage, it's this book and the fact that you are reading it!

WE NEED DAD JOKES

There is a genuine reason why we need dad jokes, perhaps more than ever. The world, especially the online world, has become increasingly polarized, hostile, and aggressive in so many areas of our lives. Beliefs and preferences have become more binary, and it increasingly feels like an 'us against them' mentality.

In a world that has become so serious and polarized, the dad joke is a very welcome break from the noise and stress. It's silly. It's unsophisticated. It's something that everyone can understand and be part of. It's an adult man making himself vulnerable and open to ridicule in the name of comic relief. It's a refreshing change from the competitive, hostile world.

THE SCIENCE BEHIND IT

Stanley Dubinsky, an English professor at the University of South Carolina, and co-author of the book Understanding Language Through Humor, enjoys ribbing his kids with dad jokes: "I take a little bit of perverse pleasure in causing them some embarrassment when I speak. Your kids have a right to be embarrassed by you anyway, so the next best thing to them laughing in earnest at your jokes is to level with that."

Dubinsky has a theory on the psychology of the dad joke: "As kids get older and less childlike, there's a sense of loss, and a nostalgia that sets in for when they were smaller. You don't have children anymore. One way to get back to that time is to go back to the stupid old jokes they used to think were funny."

Those in the field of positive psychology agree on the power of this humor. The cringe-induced eye-roll that a dad joke induces is not actually a negative reaction; it's all part of the game – an inside family joke. Your kids can sense when a dad joke is coming, and they know they have a role to play. They get to make groaning noises and say things like, "you're SO embarrassing." It's an interaction that makes them part of the joke, and it creates a playful moment between father and child.

So what actually goes on in the brain of a Dad Joke victim? In a 2016 study, published in the Laterality journal, researchers showed that the brain's left hemisphere processes the language of the pun first, while the right side takes a few moments to catch the ambiguous dual meaning. This in-between moment provides a super-awkward silence (the fun bit for dads). The instant the right side of the brain clicks, that's when the groaning begins, and the dad-joke connection has been made.

 **THE HUMAN FACTOR**

At DaddiLife, we've found that many of our favorite dad jokes are actually those that we fondly remember from our own fathers. One of our writers, Marc, recalls how his favorite is one his father used to bring out when he was a kid.

"Do you know about the famous cemetery? Everyone is dying to get in!"

"I remember rolling my eyes at that one so many times as a kid, and I used to get a little annoyed when he said it for the 100th time."

"But when I think of it now, I wish I could hear him say it one more time. I wish I could have one more opportunity to moan "daaaaad" and see that mischievous glint in his eye. It's a happy memory, and it's something I'm passing on to my kids. Somewhere up there, my dad is looking down and sharing a little chuckle every time I tell a dad joke."

Perhaps when we're all gone, our sons and daughters will one day be chatting. One will say one of our own personal favorites that will bring them fond memories of dad and a genuine chuckle. Long live the dad jokes!

PERFECTING YOUR DAD JOKE TECHNIQUE

What's the difference between a good joke and a bad joke timing.

So much of the humor is in the delivery. In fact, many comedians see the delivery as even more important than the content of the joke itself. Think about some of your favorite comedians – sometimes we know exactly what's coming, and we started giggling before the punchline comes because the timing makes it. Even if a joke itself is a certified side-splitter, get the timing wrong, and it can all fall apart. And we wouldn't want that!

To help you perfect your delivery, we spoke to the dads in the DaddiLife community for their best tips. Here are the five golden rules...

01 Keep a straight face.

The funniest jokes are those that aren't expected. If your victim thinks that you are saying something serious and important, the moment they realize you're being silly becomes that much funnier. The difference with a dad joke is that you must laugh at your own punchline once delivered.

02 *Pause for five seconds before the punchline.*

Five seconds is usually the perfect pause before delivering the punchline of a dad joke. It gives enough time for your victim to start thinking of (and dreading) the answer. A regular punchline is expected after two seconds, so that extra three seconds creates a little moment of suspense. Please note, this timing is specific for use in the delivery of dad jokes and does not pertain to regular jokes (also known as 'good jokes').

03 *Open your eyes wide at the punchline.*

When you say your embarrassing punchline, open your eyes wide as you say it. This will ensure that everyone understands that you are joking. How else would they know?

04 Know your audience, and then embarrass them.

Remember the old adage: "If a dad tells a joke, and his children aren't embarrassed by it, did he even make the joke?" When you tell your dad joke, it's essential that it's in front of as many non-family members as possible to achieve maximum humiliation (which is another word for 'success').

05 Content can be anywhere.

One of the defining factors of the classic dad joke is an element of cheese, and we don't mean Gouda! And the cheesiness comes from the content. Use whatever's in front of you. Everything is material.

Never be afraid of making dad jokes. The more you do it, the better you'll become.

Side note: Getting others involved is a sure-fire way to dad joke success. For instance, if you're out for a family dinner, making jokes to the waiter is the cornerstone of dad jokery. It is also crucial to insist that the waiter has found the jokes hilarious. Never ever stray from this position.

06 *Throw the rules out the window.*

Did you notice that this is number six of the five golden rules? Yep, it's all about not having any rules. Let your inner-funny come out in exactly the way that is authentic to you. You're one-of-a-kind, so whatever your brand of humor, whatever your style of delivery, if it's genuine, you'll be a winner! Unless you get total blank stares. In that case, revert to the five golden rules.

You're a dad, so this is your destiny! Remember, to you, they're not dad jokes; they're just... jokes.

JANUARY

DAD, DID YOU GET A HAIRCUT?
NO, I GOT THEM ALL CUT.

01

JANUARY

Why don't eggs tell jokes?
They'd crack each other up.

02

JANUARY

What do you call someone with
no nose and no body?
Nobody knows.

03

JANUARY

Why was the baby strawberry crying?
Because her parents were in a jam.

04
JANUARY

What are the strongest days of the week?
Saturday and Sunday. All the others are weekdays.

05
JANUARY

Why did the teddy bear say no to dessert?
Because she was stuffed.

06
JANUARY

What do you call a fake noodle?
An impasta.

07

JANUARY

Why did the American Football coach go
to the bank?

To get his quarter back.

08

JANUARY

What does a house always wear to a party?

Address.

09

JANUARY

Why did the kid cross the playground?

To get to the other slide.

10
JANUARY

How does a vampire start a letter?

Tomb it may concern...

11
JANUARY

Why was 6 afraid of 7?

Because 7, 8, 9.

12
JANUARY

How do you stop an astronaut's
baby from crying?

You rocket!

13

JANUARY

Why was the broom running late?

It over-swept.

14

JANUARY

What's yellow and looks like pineapple?

A lemon with a new haircut.

15

JANUARY

Why can't you trust the king of the jungle?

Because he is always lion.

16
JANUARY

What kind of music is bad for balloons?
Pop.

17
JANUARY

**A friend of mine tried to annoy me
with bird puns,**
but I soon realized that toucan play at that game.

18
JANUARY

What do you call a knight who hates fighting?
Sir Render!

19
JANUARY

Why was the computer cold?
It left its windows open.

20
JANUARY

Why are penguins socially awkward?
Because they can't break the ice.

21
JANUARY

I used to play piano by ear.
Now I use my hands.

22
JANUARY

What happened when the blue ship and the red ship collided at sea?

Their crews were marooned.

23
JANUARY

What's the best thing to put into a pie?

Your teeth!

24
JANUARY

Want to hear a long joke?

Jooooooooooooooke.

25

JANUARY

What do you call a boomerang that won't come back?
A stick.

26

JANUARY

What musical instrument is found in the bathroom? A tuba toothpaste.

27

JANUARY

What do you call a dog magician?
A labracadabrador.

28

JANUARY

What has four wheels and flies?

A garbage truck!

29

JANUARY

I told my doctor that I broke my arm in two places.

He told me to stop going there.

30
JANUARY

What do you give to a
sick lemon?

Lemon Aid!

31

JANUARY

What do you call the wife
of a hippie?

A Mississippi.

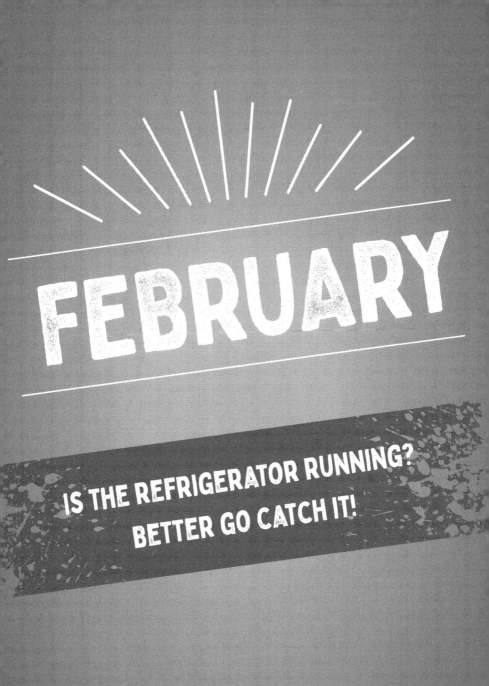

01

FEBRUARY

Did you hear the rumor about butter?

Better not spread it.

02

FEBRUARY

What's the difference between a guitar
and a fish? You can't tuna fish.

03

FEBRUARY

What did the police officer say to the
belly button?

You're under a vest.

04

FEBRUARY

What did the slow tomato say to the others?

Don't worry; I'll ketchup.

05

FEBRUARY

What gets wetter the more it dries?

A towel.

06

FEBRUARY

What did one volcano say to the other?

I lava you!

07

FEBRUARY

What do you call a guy with a rubber toe?

Roberto.

08

FEBRUARY

Why did the banana go to the doctor?

Because it wasn't peeling well.

09

FEBRUARY

Why do seagulls fly over the sea?

Because if they flew over the bay, they would be bagels.

10
FEBRUARY

How do you make an artichoke?

You strangle it.

11
FEBRUARY

Why was the sand wet?

Because the sea weed.

12
FEBRUARY

How did the baby tell her mom she had a wet diaper?

She sent her a pee-mail.

13
FEBRUARY

What kind of shoes do
private investigators wear?

Sneak-ers.

14
FEBRUARY

What do you call two birds in love?

Tweethearts!

15
FEBRUARY

Did you hear the joke about the roof?

Never mind, it's over your head.

16
FEBRUARY

Learning how to collect trash wasn't hard.

I just picked it up as I went along.

17
FEBRUARY

Why is it so windy inside a stadium?

There are hundreds of fans.

18
FEBRUARY

Why can't you trust zookeepers?

They love cheetahs.

19

FEBRUARY

What's red and bad for your teeth?

A brick.

20

FEBRUARY

What did the cupcake say to the frosting?

"I'd be muffin without you!"

21

FEBRUARY

What are bald sea captains most worried about?

Cap sizes.

FEBRUARY

What do you call a retired vegetable?
A has-bean.

FEBRUARY

Where do hamburgers go dancing?
A meatball.

FEBRUARY

What's blue and smells like red paint?
Blue paint.

25
FEBRUARY

What did one DNA strand ask the other DNA strand?

"Do these genes look OK?"

26
FEBRUARY

Why are spiders great web developers?

They like finding bugs.

27
FEBRUARY

What do cats eat for breakfast?

Mice Krispies.

28
FEBRUARY

Why do computers never fall asleep?

They're too wired.

LEAP YEAR

FEBRUARY

Did you hear the story about the claustrophobic astronaut?

He just needed some space.

MARCH

I RECENTLY DECIDED TO SELL MY VACUUM CLEANER AS ALL IT WAS DOING WAS GATHERING DUST.

01
MARCH

Why should you never trust a pig with a secret?

Because it's bound to squeal.

02
MARCH

What do you call a fish with four eyes?

Fiiiish!

03
MARCH

What kind of tree fits inyour hand?

A palm tree!

04
MARCH

What did the flower say after it told a joke?

I was just pollen your leg.

05
MARCH

Velcro

what a rip-off!

06
MARCH

Why can't Cinderella play soccer?

Because she's always running away from the ball!

07

MARCH

What did Cinderella say where her photos didn't show up? Someday my prints will come!

08

MARCH

What did the farmer call the cow that had no milk? An udder failure.

09

MARCH

How many lips does a flower have? Tu-lips.

10

MARCH

Why did the bicycle fall over?

It was two tired.

11

MARCH

Why can't you ever tell a joke around glass?

It could crack up.

12

MARCH

Where do you find a dog with no legs?

Right where you left him!

13
MARCH

Did you hear about the guy who got hit in the head with a can of soda?

He was lucky it was a soft drink.

14
MARCH

What is the smartest bird on earth?

OWL-bert Einstein.

15
MARCH

How much room should you give fungi to grow?

As mushroom as possible.

16
MARCH

Don't leave any food around your computer.

It takes a lot of bytes.

17
MARCH

What's a king's favorite kind of weather?

Reign.

18
MARCH

Did you hear about the population of Ireland?

It's Dublin.

MARCH 19

How did the barber win the race?
He knew a shortcut.

MARCH 20

What do you call a parade of rabbits hopping backward?
A receding hare-line.

MARCH 21

Why did the yogurt go to the art exhibition?
Because it was cultured.

22

MARCH

What do piggies use when they have an infection?

Antibiotic oinkment.

23

MARCH

What does Minnie Mouse drive?

A Minnie van!

24

MARCH

How does a cucumber become a pickle?

It goes through a jarring experience.

MARCH

What do knights do when they are scared of the dark?

They turn on the knight light!

MARCH

Why are elevator jokes so classic and good?

They work on many levels.

MARCH

What do you call a hen who counts her eggs?

A mathemachicken.

28
MARCH

Why do fish live in saltwater?

Because pepper makes them sneeze!

29
MARCH

What do cats wear to bed?

Paw-jamas.

30

MARCH

How does a cow
do math?

With a cow-culator.

31

MARCH

What do you get when you cross a turtle with a porcupine?

A slowpoke.

APRIL

WHAT DO YOU CALL DRACULA WITH HAYFEVER? THE POLLEN COUNT.

APRIL

Don't you hate it when someone answers their own questions?

I do.

APRIL

Why did the robber take a bath before robbing the bank?

Because he wanted to make a clean getaway!

03
APRIL

What do you call a guy that never farts in public?
A private tu-tor!

04
APRIL

Why didn't the quarter roll down the hill with the nickel?
Because it had more cents.

05
APRIL

Why did the student eat his homework?
Because the teacher told him it was a piece of cake!

06
APRIL

What time is it when the clock strikes 13?
Time to get a new clock.

07
APRIL

What kind of award did the dentist receive?
A little plaque.

08
APRIL

What did the stamp say to the envelope?
Stick with me and we'll go places!

09
APRIL

What did one hat say to the other?

"Stay here; I'm going on ahead."

10
APRIL

Where do fish keep their money?

In the riverbank.

11
APRIL

What happened after the shark got famous?

He became a starfish.

12

APRIL

What do you call a pig that does karate?

A pork chop.

13

APRIL

When do you go in red and stop on green?

When you are eating a watermelon.

14

APRIL

What did the dog say to the sandpaper?

"Ruff!"

15
APRIL

What do you call an alligator in a vest?

An investigator!

16
APRIL

What was the reporter doing
at the ice cream shop?

Getting the scoop!

17
APRIL

Which superhero is best at baseball?

Batman, of course!

18

APRIL

Why did the man buy a donkey?

Because he thought he might get a kick out of it.

19

APRIL

Did you hear about the guy whose whole left side was cut off?

He's all right now.

20

APRIL

Where do mice park their boats?

At the hickory dickory dock.

21

APRIL

Why did the banana go to the hospital?

He was peeling really bad.

22

APRIL

What did the ground say to the earthquake?

You crack me up!

23

APRIL

What did the librarian say when the books were in a mess?

We ought to be ashamed of ourshelves!

24
APRIL

Would a cardboard belt be
a waist of paper?

APRIL

When do you know when the moon has had
enough to eat?
When it's full.

APRIL

What's black and white and blue?
A depressed zebra.

27
APRIL

What did the teacher say when the horse walked into the class?

Why the long face?

28
APRIL

Did you know taller people sleep longer in bed?

29

APRIL

What's green, has six legs, and if it drops out of a tree onto you, will kill you?

A pool table.

30
APRIL

Can February March?

No, but April May!

MAY

WHAT STATE HAS A LOT
OF DOGS AND CATS?
PETS-SYLVANIA.

01
MAY

What kind of exercise do lazy people do?
Diddly-squats.

02
MAY

What did the little corn say to the mama corn?
Where is pop corn?

03
MAY

Where do rabbits go after they get married?
On a bunny-moon!

04
MAY

How does Darth Vader like his toast?

On the dark side.

05
MAY

What is a tornado's favorite game to play?

Twister!

06
MAY

Who was Socrates' worst student?

Mediocrities.

07

MAY

What do frogs like to drink?

Diet croak.

08

MAY

Why did the computer go to the dentist?

It had a blue tooth.

09

MAY

What do baseball players eat on?

Home plates!

10
MAY

What kind of chicken is the funniest?

A comedi-hen!

11
MAY

What do you call Chewbacca with cookies in its fur?

A chocolate-chip Wookie.

12
MAY

Where should a dog never go shopping?

A flea market.

13
MAY

Why did the piano teacher need a ladder?

To reach the high notes!

14
MAY

I heard a funny joke about a boomerang earlier.

I'm sure it'll come back to me eventually.

15
MAY

What do you call a blind dinosaur?

A Doyouthinkhesawus.

16
MAY

What do you get if you cross fireworks
with a duck?

Firequacker!

17
MAY

Never lie to an x-ray technician.

They can see right through you.

18
MAY

When is a baby good at basketball?

When it's dribbling!

19
MAY

I'm working on a device that will read minds.

I'd love to hear your thoughts.

20
MAY

What do you call a man in a pile of leaves?

Russell.

21
MAY

What did the tree wear to the pool party?

Swimming trunks!

22
MAY

What goes zzub zzub?
A bee flying backwards!

23
MAY

When should you buy a chicken?
When it's going cheep!

24
MAY

What is a snake's favorite subject?
Hiss-tory!

MAY

What does a skeleton say before he eats?

Bone Appetit!

MAY

What did the Atlantic Ocean say to the Indian Ocean?

Try to be more Pacific!

MAY

What do you call a monkey at the North Pole?

Lost.

28
MAY

What do you call a guy with
a seagull on his head?
Cliff.

29
MAY

What do snowmen call their
fancy annual dance?
The Snowball.

30
MAY

What's small and red and has
a rough voice?

A hoarse raddish!

31
MAY

What's orange and sounds
like a parrot.

A carrot.

JUNE

WHAT DID THE DIGITAL CLOCK SAY TO THE GRANDFATHER CLOCK? LOOK! NO HANDS!

01

JUNE

What do ghosts like to eat in the summer?

I Scream.

02

JUNE

Why was the burglar so sensitive?

He takes things personally.

03

JUNE

What is black and white and looks
like a penguin?

A penguin.

04
JUNE

Why do we say "break a leg" to actors?

Because every play needs a cast!

05
JUNE

What cheese is made backwards?

Edam.

06
JUNE

Where do polar bears vote?

The North Poll.

07
JUNE

What do lawyers wear to court?

Lawsuits!

08
JUNE

Why was the picture sent to jail?

It was framed.

09
JUNE

How did Benjamin Franklin feel when he discovered electricity?

Shocked!

10
JUNE

Which hand is better to write with?

Neither, it's better to write with a pen.

11
JUNE

Why did the golfer wear two pairs of pants?

Just in case he got a hole in one.

12
JUNE

What happens when it rains cats and dogs?

You can step into a poodle.

13
JUNE

I was struggling to figure out how lightning works.
Then it struck me.

14
JUNE

Why did the poor dog chase his own tail?
He was trying to make both ends meet!

15
JUNE

I have a speed bump phobia,
but I'm slowly getting over it.

16

JUNE

How do you cut the sea in half?

With a sea saw!

17

JUNE

How do trees get on the internet?

They log in!

18

JUNE

What do you call a guy lying on your doorstep?

Matt.

JUNE 19

Where do young cows eat lunch?

In the calf-ateria.

JUNE 20

What's a vampire's favorite fruit?

A neck-tarine!

JUNE 21

Where did the school kittens
go for their field trip?

To the mew-seum.

22
JUNE

What do you call two witches living together?

Broommates.

23
JUNE

Where does the sheep get his hair cut?

The baa baa shop!

24
JUNE

Why did the police arrest the turkey?

They suspected it of fowl play.

25
JUNE

Where do kings keep their armies?
In their sleevies!

26
JUNE

Which part of the car has the most fun?
The WHEEEEEls!

27
JUNE

I saw an ad for burial plots,
and thought to myself,
this is the last thing I need.

28
JUNE

What does a sea monster eat?

Fish and Ships!

29
JUNE

What do you call a lady with one leg longer than the other?

Eileen.

30
JUNE

Sue broke her finger today, but on the other hand she was completely fine.

JULY

SOMEBODY ACTUALLY COMPLIMENTED ME ON MY DRIVING TODAY. THEY LEFT A LITTLE NOTE, IT SAID 'PARKING FINE.'

01
JULY

Where do pencils go on vacation?
Pencil-vania.

02
JULY

Why aren't dogs good dancers?
They have two left feet.

03
JULY

What did the pirate say on his 80th birthday?
Aye matey.

04
JULY

Last night, I dreamed I was swimming in an ocean of orange soda.

But it was just a Fanta sea.

05
JULY

At what sport do waiters do so well?

Tennis, because they're really good at serving.

06
JULY

What did the beach say as the tide came in?

Long time, no sea.

07
JULY

Why are cats so good at video games?
Because they have nine lives.

08
JULY

What did Venus say to Saturn?
"Give me a ring sometime!"

09
JULY

What did the clock ask the watch?
Hour you doing?

10
JULY

When it comes to cosmetic surgery,
a lot of people turn their noses up.

11
JULY

I'm an archaeologist.
My career is in ruins.

12
JULY

What do you call two monkeys sharing an Amazon account?
PRIME-mates.

13
JULY

What do cows read?

CATTLE-logs.

14
JULY

Why did the turkey cross the road twice?

To show he wasn't a chicken.

15
JULY

What do you call a manwith 100 rabbits?

Warren.

16
JULY

How much is the moon worth?
One dollar, because it has four quarters.

17
JULY

What did the grape say when it was stepped on?
Nothing, it just let out a little wine.

18
JULY

Where do you learn to make ice cream?
Sundae school.

19
JULY

A burger walks into a bar.
The bartender says,
'Sorry, we don't serve food here.'

20
JULY

How does the moon cut his hair?
Eclipse it!

21
JULY

My dolphin puns are terrible
on porpoise.

JULY

I'm reading a book about anti-gravity.

I can't put it down.

23
JULY

What do Olympic sprinters eat before a race?

Nothing. They fast.

JULY

Found out I was color blind the other day.

That one came right out of the orange.

25

JULY

Once you've seen one shopping center,
you've seen the mall.

26

JULY

What do you call a bee that can't make up
its mind? A maybe.

27

JULY

What sits at the bottom of the sea
and twitches?

A nervous wreck.

28
JULY

A man tells his doctor, "Doc, help me. I'm addicted to Twitter!" The doctor replies, "Sorry, I don't follow you ..."

29
JULY

A soldier survived mustard gas in battle, and then pepper spray by the police. He's now a seasoned veteran.

30

JULY

My friend says to me:
"What rhymes with orange?"
I said: "No it doesn't!"

31

JULY

My grandfather invented the cold air balloon.

It never really took off.

AUGUST

WHERE DO SHEEP GO ON VACATION? THE BAAA-HAMAS

01

AUGUST

What is brown, hairy, and wears sunglasses?

A coconut on vacation.

02

AUGUST

Two pickles fell out of a jar onto the floor.

What did one say to the other? Dill with it.

03

AUGUST

What do you get when you cross an elephant with a fish?

Swimming trunks.

04
AUGUST

What sound do you hear when a cow breaks the sound barrier? Cowboom!

05
AUGUST

What does bread do on vacation?
Loaf around.

06
AUGUST

If you take your watch to be fixed,
make sure you don't pay upfront.
Wait until the time is right.

AUGUST

What did the one toilet say to the other?

You look a bit flushed.

AUGUST

What do you call a pile of cats?

A meow-tain.

AUGUST

What event do spiders love to attend?

Webbings.

10
AUGUST

Why is a leopard so bad at hiding?

Because he's always spotted.

11
AUGUST

What's the best way to communicate with fish?

Drop them a line.

12
AUGUST

What's in the recipe for gold soup?

Fourteen carrots!

13
AUGUST

What type of songs do the planets sing?
Nep-tunes!

14
AUGUST

Why do bowling pins have such a hard life?
They're always getting knocked down.

15
AUGUST

I bet the butcher the other day that he couldn't reach the meat that was on the top shelf.
He refused to take the bet, saying that the steaks were too high.

16
AUGUST

A cement mixer collided with a prison van.
Motorists are asked to be on the lookout for 16 hardened criminals.

17
AUGUST

I'm addicted to brake fluid,
but I can stop whenever I want.

18
AUGUST

What did the bald man say when he received a
comb for a present?

"Thanks! I'll never part with it!"

19
AUGUST

Where are average things manufactured?

The satisfactory.

20

AUGUST

What's a cow's favorite drink?

A s-moooo-thie.

21

AUGUST

Why do bees have sticky hair?

Because they use honeycombs!

22

AUGUST

I once had a teacher with a lazy eye.

She couldn't control her pupils.

23

AUGUST

A slice of apple pie is $2.50 in Jamaica and £$ in the Bahamas...There are the pie rates of the Caribbean.

24

AUGUST

I started a band called 999 megabytes...
We still haven't gotten a gig.

25

AUGUST

I just found out my friend has a secret life as a priest... It's his altar ego.

26
AUGUST

What do dogs do when they need a break while watching a movie?

They put it on paws.

27
AUGUST

Why can't T-Rexes clap their hands?

Because they are extinct.

28
AUGUST

If anyone knows how to fix some broken hinges,

my door's always open.

AUGUST 29

Did you hear about the giant who threw up?

It's all over town.

AUGUST 30

Do you have holes in your underwear?

No? So how do you put your
legs through?

30
AUGUST

What did the frog order at McDonald's?

French flies and Diet Croak.

SEPTEMBER

I'LL CALL YOU LATER. DON'T CALL ME LATER, CALL ME DAD!

01
SEPTEMBER

What is a witch's favorite subject in school?
Spelling!

02
SEPTEMBER

How does a scientist freshen her breath?
With experi-mints!

03
SEPTEMBER

How can you tell a vampire has a cold?
He starts coffin.

04
SEPTEMBER

What is a computer's favorite snack?

Computer chips!!

05
SEPTEMBER

What do elves learn in school?

The elf-abet.

06
SEPTEMBER

What be the pirate's favorite letter of the alphabet?

Arrrr!

SEPTEMBER

I tried to sue the airport for misplacing my **luggage.** I lost my case.

SEPTEMBER

What starts with E, ends with E, and has only 1 letter in it?
An envelope.

SEPTEMBER

What did the paper say to the pencil?
Write on!

10

SEPTEMBER

What's an astronaut's favorite meal?

Launch!

11

SEPTEMBER

What did the janitor say when he jumped
out of the closet?

SUPPLIES!

12

SEPTEMBER

Why did the dog do so well in school?

Because he was the teacher's pet!

13

SEPTEMBER

So a lorry-load of tortoises crashed into a trainload of terrapins, I thought, 'That's a turtle disaster.'

14

SEPTEMBER

I once had to break up with this girl who just would not stop counting.
I wonder what she's up to now.

15

SEPTEMBER

Bread is like the Sun.
Rises in the yeast, sets in the waist.

16
SEPTEMBER

A man threw a block of cheese at me in the supermarket. How dairy.

17
SEPTEMBER

I gave up my seat to a blind person on the bus. That's how I lost my job as a bus driver.

18
SEPTEMBER

How do you get a tissue to dance? You put a boogie in it.

19
SEPTEMBER

Know why they use knots instead of miles in the ocean?

Because they've got to keep the ocean tide.

20
SEPTEMBER

There are only 3 types of people...

1. People who can count   2. People who can't

21
SEPTEMBER

The all vegetable circus came to town yesterday.

I hear their clown act is corny.

 142

SEPTEMBER

What's a Pokémon that sneezes a lot?
Pik-Hachoo.

SEPTEMBER

While shopping for school supplies, I came across a pen that can write underwater. It can write other words as well.

SEPTEMBER

Bowling jokes are right up
my alley.

25

SEPTEMBER

I saw a man at the beach yelling, "Help, shark!"
Which was so weird. If I needed help, a shark
would be the last thing I call for.

26

SEPTEMBER

What's a pet fish's favorite holiday?
Tanksgiving.

27

SEPTEMBER

Don't make an origami belt.
It's a waist of paper.

28
SEPTEMBER

Have you heard about the chocolate record player? It sounds pretty sweet.

SEPTEMBER

Where do fruits go on vacation?" "Pear-is!

SEPTEMBER

I don't trust stairs. They're always up to something.

OCTOBER

I SAW AN ADVERT THAT READ: "TELEVISION FOR SALE, $1, VOLUME STUCK ON FULL." I THOUGHT TO MYSELF, I CAN'T TURN THAT DOWN.

01
OCTOBER

What kind of music do mummies love?
Wrap music.

02
OCTOBER

What do you call a ghost's true love?
His ghoul-friend.

03
OCTOBER

Why did the orange lose the race?
because he ran out of juice.

04

OCTOBER

What did the banana say to the dog?

Nothing. Bananas can't talk.

05

OCTOBER

Why are ghosts bad liars?

Because you can see right through them.

06

OCTOBER

Why did the teacher wear sunglasses to school?

Because her students were so bright.

07
OCTOBER

What is more impressive than a talking parrot?
A spelling bee.

08
OCTOBER

How do poets say hello?
Hey, haven't we metaphor?

09
OCTOBER

If I got 50 cents for every failed math exam,
I'd have $ 6.30 now.

10
OCTOBER

Why did Humpty Dumpty have a great fall?
To make up for his miserable summer.

11
OCTOBER

What does a cloud wear under his raincoat?
Thunderwear.

12
OCTOBER

A man who runs behind a car will get exhausted,
but a man who runs in front of a car will get tired.

13
OCTOBER

What's the scariest plant?

Bam-booo!

14
OCTOBER

What time do ducks wake up?

At the quack of dawn.

15
OCTOBER

What do elves do after school?

Their gnome work.

16
OCTOBER

What room doesn't have doors?

A mushroom.

17
OCTOBER

Did you hear about the actor who fell through the floorboards?

He was just going through a stage.

18

OCTOBER

What do kids play when they can't play
with a phone?
Bored games.

19

OCTOBER

**I told your mother I was going to make a bike
out of spaghetti.** You should have seen her face
when I rode straight pasta!

20

OCTOBER

My favorite time on a clock is 6:30.

Hands down.

21

OCTOBER

I used to be a personal trainer.

Then I gave my too weak notice.

22

OCTOBER

What do you call two witches living together?

Broommates.

23
OCTOBER

How does a penguin build its house?

Igloos it together.

24
OCTOBER

What concert costs just 45 cents?

50 Cent featuring Nickelback!

25
OCTOBER

What do you call a shoe made of a banana?

A slipper!

26
OCTOBER

"Dad, can you put my shoes on?"
"No, I don't think they'll fit me."

27
OCTOBER

Why can't kids remember past birthdays?
Because they're too focused on the present.

28
OCTOBER

What does a lemon say when it answers
the phone?"
"Yellow!

29

OCTOBER

What's a cat's favorite type
of Mexican food?

Purritos.

30

OCTOBER

I ordered a chicken and an
egg from Amazon.

I'll let you know...

31

OCTOBER

What time did the man go
to the dentist?

Tooth Hurty!

NOVEMBER

I GOT MY DAUGHTER A FRIDGE FOR HER BIRTHDAY. I CAN'T WAIT TO SEE HER FACE LIGHT UP WHEN SHE OPENS IT.

01
NOVEMBER

How do you get a squirrel to like you?

Act like a nut!

02
NOVEMBER

What dinosaur had the best vocabulary?

The thesaurus.

03
NOVEMBER

What do you get when you cross a vampire
and a snowman?

Frost bite!

04
NOVEMBER

What do you call an elephant that doesn't matter?

An irrelephant.

05
NOVEMBER

Why should you stand in the corner if you get cold?

It's always 90 degrees.

06
NOVEMBER

Why is peter pan always flying?

He neverlands.

NOVEMBER 07

Did you hear about the boy who tried to catch fog?

He mist.

NOVEMBER 08

I went to buy some camouflage trousers the **other day,** but I couldn't find any.

NOVEMBER 09

How do modern-day pirates keep in touch?

SEA-mail.

10
NOVEMBER

What do you call a man with a shovel?

Doug.

11
NOVEMBER

Who is the most famous fish spy?

James Pond.

12
NOVEMBER

Did you hear about the coin factory that
stopped working?

It doesn't make any cents.

13
NOVEMBER

What did the fish say when he hit the wall?
Dam.

14
NOVEMBER

Did you hear about the famous pickle?
He was a big dill!

15
NOVEMBER

Why is it a bad idea to iron your four-leaf clover? Cause you shouldn't press your luck.

16
NOVEMBER

Why do melons have weddings?
Because they cantaloupe!

17
NOVEMBER

How many apples grow on a tree?
All of them!

18
NOVEMBER

Last night I had a dream that I weighed less
than a thousandth of a gram.
I was like, 0 mg.

NOVEMBER

A cheese factory exploded in France.

Da brie is everywhere!

NOVEMBER

I was really angry at my friend Mark for stealing my dictionary.

I told him, "Mark, my words!"

NOVEMBER

Why do dogs float in water?

Because they are good buoys.

22
NOVEMBER

What's ET short for?

Because he's only got tiny legs!

23
NOVEMBER

Why couldn't the green pepper practice archery?

Because it didn't habanero.

24
NOVEMBER

What do you call a sad cup of coffee?

Depresso.

NOVEMBER

Not to brag, but I made six figures last year.
I was also named worst employee at the toy factory.

NOVEMBER

My boss told me to have a good day,
so I went home!

NOVEMBER

I used to run a dating service for chickens.
But I was struggling to make hens meet.

28
NOVEMBER

I accidentally dropped my pillow on the floor.

I think it has a concushion.

29
NOVEMBER

Did you hear about the ATM that got addicted to money?

It suffered from withdrawals.

30
NOVEMBER

Why did the scarecrow win an award?

Because he was outstanding in his field.

DECEMBER

WHAT DO YOU CALL
AN OLD SNOWMAN?
WATER.

01
DECEMBER

The world tongue-twister champion just got arrested. I hear they're gonna give him a really tough sentence.

02
DECEMBER

What is a cat's favorite color? Purrr-ple!

03
DECEMBER

What do you get when you combine a Christmas tree with an iPad?
A pineapple.

04
DECEMBER

What is a ghost's favorite position in soccer?
Ghoul Keeper!

05
DECEMBER

Where does the T-rex go shopping?
The dino store!

06
DECEMBER

Where do horses live?
In neighhh-borhoods.

07

DECEMBER

What do you call a droid that takes the
long way around?
R2 detour.

08

DECEMBER

What do you call a reindeer with bad manners?
Rude-olph.

09

DECEMBER

What kind of photos do elves take?
Elfies.

10

DECEMBER

What do you call a poor Santa Claus?

"St. Nickel-less."

11

DECEMBER

I'm on a seafood diet.

I see food and I eat it.

12

DECEMBER

I never buy pre-shredded cheese.

Because doing it yourself is grate.

13
DECEMBER

Why don't crabs give to charity?
Because they're shellfish.

14
DECEMBER

I have a great joke about nepotism.
But I'll only tell it to my kids.

15
DECEMBER

Hear about the new restaurant called Karma? There's no menu —you get what you deserve.

16

DECEMBER

What do you call 50 pigs and 50 deer?

100 sows and bucks.

17

DECEMBER

Why do cows wear bells?

Because their horns don't work.

18

DECEMBER

What do you call a lazy kangaroo?

Pouch potato.

19
DECEMBER

A steak pun is a rare
medium done well.

20
DECEMBER

What's a bad wizard's favorite
computer program? Spell-check.

21
DECEMBER

Did you hear that Arnold Schwarzenegger will
be doing a movie about classical music?
He'll be Bach.

22
DECEMBER

Why shouldn't you give Elsa a balloon?
Because she'll let it go!

23
DECEMBER

How do you make holy water?
You boil the hell out of it.

24
DECEMBER

What's every parent's favorite Christmas Carol?
Silent Night.

25

DECEMBER

What does Santa suffer from if he gets stuck in a chimney? Claustrophobia.

26

DECEMBER

What do snowmen call their offspring?
Chill-dren

27

DECEMBER

What's the difference between a poorly dressed man on a tricycle and a well-dressed man on a bicycle? Attire.

28
DECEMBER

What's every elf's favorite type of music?

Wrap.

29
DECEMBER

What's green, covered in tinsel, and goes 'ribbet ribbet'?

A Mistle-toad.

30
DECEMBER

What's black and white and goes around and around?

A penguin in a revolving door.

31

DECEMBER

When does a joke become a
dad joke?

When it becomes apparent.

CONCLUSION

What's black and white and red all over? This book...or a sunburnt Zebra!

We hope you've enjoyed this compilation of dad jokes. If you've reached this point because you've terrorized your family 365 times (or 366 times if you're reading this in a leap year), well done!

We hope it's brought you and your family closer. When you see the weary faces of your children, remember that these moments of silliness will be remembered fondly one day. Out of the 366 dad jokes, a few may even be passed onto their own children one day. If you've skipped to this part and are yet to get started, jump in! There's no time better than the present. Every parent is shocked at how quickly their kids grow up. If you have young children, treat every moment like it's gold. Don't wait too long before you make your whole family cringe and moan. It's surprisingly satisfying!

If you enjoyed this book, please take a moment to leave a review. And don't forget to tell us which joke was your favorite!

One last question...

How do you keep an idiot in suspense?

OUR GIFT

TWO SPECIAL GIFTS FOR OUR READERS

AS A SPECIAL THANK YOU FOR GETTING THIS BOOK, WE'D LIKE TO GIVE YOU:

New Message

To: theluckyreader@message.com

Subject: Dad Joke of the Day!

WHY DID THE GOLFER CHANGE HIS PANTS?

BECAUSE HE GOT A HOLE IN ONE!

A BONUS MONTH OF DAD JOKES

AN EXTRA 31 DAYS WORTH OF DAD JOKES, DELIVERED STRAIGHT TO YOUR INBOX FOR YOU TO USE ON YOUR UNSUSPECTING VICTIM!

A BOOK EXCLUSIVE (AVAILABLE ONLY WITH THIS BOOK)

THE SURPRISING PSYCHOLOGY OF LAUGHTER, AND 10 UNIQUE TOOLS & TECHNIQUES FOR YOU TO MAKE LAUGHTER AN EVERYDAY HABIT FOR THE FAMILY

A LAUGH A DAY

VISIT WWW.DADDILIFE.COM/LOL TO GET YOURS!

ACKNOWLEDGEMENTS

massive thank you to the DaddiLife writers – especially Marc, Hugh, Michael, and Jon for their countless hours of inspiration and good humor in putting this book together.

A very special thank you too to Emilie Dorange and Jon Shortt. Emilie in particular for her design wizardry, and Jon in particular for his absolutely amazing illustrations that we've enjoyed laughing at more than we should have!